Beginning Fun With
Water & Bubbles

Written by Gayle Bittinger
Illustrated by Marion Hopping Ekberg

Totline® Publications
A Division of Frank Schaffer Publications, Inc.
Torrance, California

Editorial Manager: Kathleen Cubley
Contributing Editors: Carol Gnojewski, Susan Hodges,
  Elizabeth McKinnon, Jean Warren
Copyeditor: Kris Fulsaas
Proofreader: Miriam Bulmer
Editorial Assistant: Durby Peterson
Graphic Designer (cover): Brenda Mann Harrison
Graphic Designer: Sarah Ness
Production Manager: Melody Olney

ISBN 1-57029-151-9

Printed in the United States of America
Published by Totline® Publications
Editorial Office: P.O. Box 2250
              Everett, WA 98203
Business Office: 23740 Hawthorne Blvd.
              Torrance, CA 90505

20 19 18 17 16 15 14 13 12 11 10 9 8 7 6 5 4 3 2

Water fascinates young children.

Water play is one of the most interesting and absorbing activities for young children. Without even realizing it, they become scientists as they explore what happens when they do this, what the water does in this container, how many spoonfuls it takes to fill up this cup, and so on. And when you add bubbles to the water, the exploration begins all over again.

You and your child will discover all sorts of water activities in this book: water toys to make to explore water, what water does when it gets cold or when it gets hot, and more. Together, you will also find many activities for exploring bubbles—recipes for making homemade bubble solution, bubble wands you can make at home, and ways to have fun with bubbles. Continue the exploration as you think of new ways to explore water and bubbles together.

Bubbles Up!

A Word About Safety: The activities in *Beginning Fun With Water and Bubbles* are appropriate for young children between the ages of 2 and 5. However, keep in mind that if a project calls for using small objects, an adult should supervise at all times to make sure that children do not put the objects in their mouth. It is recommended that you use art materials that are specifically labeled as safe for children unless the materials are to be used only by an adult.

Water Exploration

Let your child explore water to her heart's content. Fill a sink with water, provide a step stool, and let your child play. Or, if you prefer, place a plastic dishpan (or a plastic bathtub for infants) on a towel and fill it partway with water. Give your child some plastic cups and spoons and let her explore. Remind her to keep the water in the sink or the tub. (An apron will help keep her dry.) Talk about what the water does: it pours, it splashes, it fills up cups, and so on.

For More Fun

Change the water in the tub to provide new opportunities for discovery. Put warm water in the sink or the dishpan; add a few drops of dishwashing detergent and a whisk to make bubbles. Or add a drop or two of food coloring to color the water (it won't color hands!).

Ice Floats

Let your child help you select several plastic containers for making ice. Fill the containers most of the way with water and put them in the freezer for several hours. (If you wish, you can also add a drop or two of food coloring to each container.) Fill a sink with warm water and add the ice from the containers. Ask your child to notice what happens to the ice. Does it floak or sink? What happens when he runs warm water on the ice? Can he make a hole in the ice? Let him continue this exploration of warm water and cold ice.

Holes for Water

Collect several identical plastic cups, such as small yogurt containers. Turn the cups upside down and, using a nail, poke one hole in the first container, two holes in the second container, and so on. Fill a sink or a dishpan with water. Give your child the cups and let her explore with them. Which cup holds water the longest? Which cup makes the best shower?

For More Fun

Give your child one cup with no holes in it. Help her find out which one of the "holey" cups fills up the plain cup the fastest.

Sponge Fun

When your child is taking a bath, give him several sponges to play with. Help him figure out how to fill the sponge with water and how to squeeze the water out. Does each sponge hold the same amount of water? What happens when a dry or "squeezed-out" sponge is put in the water? Can he see the bubbles coming out from the sponge? What is doing that? (The air in the sponge is being pushed out by the water and comes out as air bubbles.)

For More Fun

Purchase miniature sponges that expand when put into water (available at toy stores and some kitchen stores). Your child will love watching them in action.

Evaporation Experiment

Introduce your child to the concept of evaporation (the process of water molecules
heating up and becoming vapor in the
air). On a sunny day, give your child a
bucket of water and a paintbrush. Take
her outside to "paint" the sidewalk, a
fence, or another surface. Have her notice
the water marks she leaves as she paints.
In a short while, have her look back
at the areas she has painted. Is the
water still there? Explain that the
water has evaporated—the sun
has heated up the water
and it has become
vapor in the air.

For More Fun

Evaporation is also why wet
clothes eventually dry out.
Let your child discover
which fabrics dry out fastest
with this experiment. Provide squares of several different kinds of fabric, such
as terry cloth, cotton, wool,
and denim. Let your child
soak all of them in water
and wring them out. Help
her hang the fabric from a
clothesline. Encourage her
to check the fabrics through-
out the day to see which
ones dry fastest.

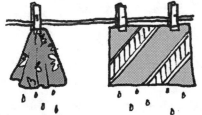

Condensation Experiment

Let your child fill a jar with cold water and add some ice cubes. Put a lid on the jar and set it out on a table. Ask him to predict what is going to happen to the outside of the jar. Will it get cold? Will it stay dry? Have him check the jar a little while later. What does he notice about the outside of the jar? (It is cold and wet.) Where did the water come from? Explain that the water on the outside of the jar came from the air. When the water in the air gets cold, it forms water droplets called condensation.

Bubbles and Bubble Wands

Bubble Solutions

Purchased bubble solutions are easy to use and come in their own small containers, and there is nothing quite like the thrill of a brand-new bottle of bubbles. However, it is possible to make your own bubble solutions, often at a fraction of the cost of purchased ones.

Simple Bubble Mix—This bubble solution is similar to the kind you can buy. In a container with a lid, mix together 1/4 cup Joy brand dishwashing detergent (other brands do not work as well), 1/2 cup water, a few drops of food coloring, and 1 teaspoon sugar. Put the lid on and let this mixture age for two to three days before using it.

Gooey Bubble Mix—This mixture is great for toddlers and for blowing huge bubbles because it stays together so well. However, it does have the disadvantage of making the ground slippery wherever the bubbles pop. Mix together 1 cup Joy brand dishwashing detergent (other brands do not work as well), 3 cups water, and 6 tablespoons light corn syrup. Let the solution sit for a few hours before using.

Using Bubble Solution

Bubble solution often ends up all over the ground as your child tips over the container in excitement. You can purchase bubble containers that will virtually eliminate spills. However, there are some homemade solutions that will slow down bubble spills and make bubble play easier for your child. (Of course, playing with bubbles outside is the first step to making any potential mess easier to clean up.)

Bubble Cup—If your child is using a small bubble wand, put bubble solution in a small yogurt container, snap on the lid, and cut a slit in the lid, large enough for the wand to fit through.

Bubble Pan—Large bubble wands work best when they can be dipped completely into bubble solution. Find a large, rectangular plastic storage container with a removable, snap-on lid. Place the container, without its lid, on the ground or a low surface. Fill the pan with about 1 inch of bubble solution. This is enough for dipping the bubble wand, but not so much that if it spills it will be too disappointing. When you are done, snap on the lid and store it until the next time.

Making Bubble Wands
There are beautiful bubble wands that you can purchase, but there are also many other unique bubble wands you can make from ordinary household objects.

Hanger—A child-size plastic clothes hanger makes a perfect bubble wand for a young child. Have him hold onto the handle, dip the hanger into the bubble solution, and run. Big, beautiful bubbles will stream out behind him. (This wand works especially well with the Gooey Bubble Mix.)

Berry Basket—A plastic berry basket makes wonderful tiny bubbles. Have your child dip the bottom or the side of the basket in bubble solution and spin around in circles to make a ribbon of bubbles.

Funnel—Show your child how to dip the wide of a funnel into bubble solution, then blow through the narrow end to make a big bubble.

Pipe Cleaner—Bend a pipe cleaner into any desired shape, such as a heart, a star, or a diamond, leaving an end for a handle. Let your child hold the shape by the handle. Have her dip it into the bubble solution and then blow through the open shape to make bubbles.

Pop! Go the Bubbles

Take your child outside. Have her point to her elbows. Tell her that you are going to blow some bubbles and that she can use only her elbows to pop them. Blow the bubbles and let your child begin popping them. How many can she pop with her elbows? Is it easier or harder than popping them with her hands? Now, let your child blow bubbles for you to pop with your elbows. Repeat, choosing a different body part for popping the bubbles.

Bubble Song

Sing the following song with your child while you blow bubbles together and then try to pop them all.

Sung to: "Frére Jacques"

Bubbles floating, bubbles floating
In the air, in the air.
See them floating here,
See them floating there,
Everywhere, in the air.

Bubbles popping, bubbles popping
In the air, in the air.
See them popping here,
See them popping there,
Everywhere, in the air.

Gayle Bittinger

Bubble Prints

Your child will love the art she creates with this special painting technique. In a small bowl, gently mix together 1 tablespoon tempera paint, 2 tablespoons liquid dishwashing detergent, and 4 tablespoons water. Give your child a plastic drinking straw. Have her practice blowing out through the straw (not breathing or sucking in). When she has mastered blowing out, have her put the straw into the paint mixture and blow through it *gently* until a mound of bubbles forms over the top of the bowl. Help her place a sheet of white paper over the bubbles. The bubbles will pop, leaving delicate designs on the paper. Repeat as many times as you and your child wish.

Parent Resources
from Totline® Publications

Beginning Fun With Art

Creative ideas that use ordinary materials. Perfect for introducing a young child to the fun of art while developing coordination skills and building self-confidence.

Scissors • Yarn • Paint • Modeling Dough • Glue • Stickers • Craft Sticks • Crayons • Felt • Paper Shapes • Rubber Stamps • Tissue Paper

Learning Everywhere

These books present ideas for turning ordinary moments into teaching opportunities. You'll find ways to spend fun, quality time with your child while you lay the foundation for language, art, science, math, problem solving, and building self-esteem.

Teaching House • Teaching Town Teaching Trips

A Year of Fun

Hang up these age-specific resource guides for great advice on child development, practical parenting, and age-appropriate activities that jump-start learning.

**Just for Babies
Just for Ones
Just for Twos
Just for Threes
Just for Fours
Just for Fives**

Getting Ready for School

Use these five valuable books to show you how to help your child develop the skills necessary for school success. The activities combine ordinary materials with simple instructions for fun at home that leads to learning.

Ready to Learn Colors, Shapes, and Numbers • Ready to Write and Develop Motor Skills • Ready to Read • Ready to Communicate • Ready to Listen and Explore the Senses

Car Wash

Help your child set up a bubbly "car wash" for his outdoor riding toys. You will need a bucket of soapy water, a sponge, a bucket of clean water or a hose with a trigger-type nozzle, and an old towel or a rag for drying. Let him soap up his riding toys, scrub them with the sponge, rinse them with clean water, and dry them off with the towel for immediate riding. You can also include other outdoor toys in this cleaning frenzy.

For More Fun
Let your child help you make signs for your car wash and invite neighborhood children over for a giant, do-it-yourself car wash.